MW01594844

Career And Salary Guide
Do You Want To Find High Paying
Jobs?
Are You Paid At Market Rates?

Comprehensive Guide to Check
Market Salaries for 60 Professions

William J King

Classic and Digital Publishing, LLC
Cheyenne, WY

Disclaimer:

While every care has been taken in compiling the details and links, the author and publisher is not responsible for the contents. Please make sure you verify from several sources before you undertake any changes from your current state. Salary is a complex issue and will depend on several factors, one of which is Market Salaries. The author and publisher do not take responsibility for the accuracy of the contents

©2015 Classic and Digital Publishing, LLC

Cover illustration Liana

All rights reserved. No portion of this book may be used without the sole permission of the copyright holder except in use of a review.

Published by Classic and Digital Publishing, LLC

Some of the links (excluding any and all links to Amazon.com) in this e-book may be "affiliate links". This means if you click on the link and purchase the item, I may receive commission. Please understand I only recommend products or services I use personally and believe will add value to my readers. I am disclosing this in accordance with Federal Trade Commission's 16 CFR, Part 255: "Guides Concerning the Use of Endorsements and Testimonials."

Check out all of William's books at WilliamJkingonline.com and get additional resources!

FREE BONUS

Quick Start Guide to Saving $3K a year

This is a "Quick start guide" for a book that I wrote for "Savings made easy". Usually we don't take action right away. This guide will help you take actions today and you will be on your way to saving $3K this year. You can download it for FREE at WilliamJKingonline.com

Contents

Comparative Salaries for 60 Occupations in the United States

Money may not be able to buy happiness. However, when it comes to choosing a career it does make a huge difference. Unless someone is independently wealthy, they are very concerned about possible earnings in their desired field. This is true for career explorers as well as those already in a career field. Because of this fact there a multitude of sites that offer salary information. This includes the federal government whose Bureau of Labor Statistics specializes in tracking salary information.

Finding the information, you need to compare salaries across the United States can be overwhelming. We cover some of the most popular, and often highest paying, career fields that people explore. Each site has done a great job of assembling information about salary in these jobs. That data is organized into different categories Sources for this information come from the Bureau of Labor Statistics, trade organizations, and various surveys. This has a comprehensive list of websites that offer valuable information on salaries in the top 60 careers.

Careers

Careers and Salary expectations go hand in hand. Information on salaries for over 60 job categories are available in this resource guide. While there are no guarantees on what an employer will ultimately pay you, which could depend on several factors, it is smart to understand what the market salaries are. Skim through all the chapters, then go to the websites to understand salaries better. Never make a decision based on one resource. Go through a wide variety of options before taking any decision.

Easy Steps to Get a Raise at Work

Many things affect your earnings potential. For those of you who commit to a specific company, the question of being paid more salary can be complicated. If your job is reliable, and pays well 'enough,' then you often avoid the effort of asking for a good raise. Some companies neglect workers if they believe that they are fully committed to the company. They assume that they will remain, even if their annual raises or bonuses don't match the rate of inflation. Nevertheless, there are a number of good strategies to use when asking for a raise from a good employer.

Not everyone is in the position to receive a big raise. Some employees are members of organized labor unions, which means that big adjustments in earnings are set by the contracts negotiated between union and management. Others are government employees, whose salaries are set by laws and government regulations.

However, for those of whose earnings are not so structured, there are specific strategies that can help structure the conversation to your advantage. And beyond this, it should be possible for you to increase your own raise potential above even the average annual basic raise simply by following a few simple pieces of advice.

The most important tactic here is planning. Those employees who best prepare their bosses' minds for the requested raise will have the advantage. It's very simple, but sometimes this will still require advance planning.

Planning should leave very little to chance. You should know each stage of the "how to acquire a big raise" process. The first step is to confirm the regular income range for your type of work, and for your area of the country. There is no sense in requesting a raise that is not well-matched to the job you do or where you live. But when you are able to prove that you are paid below the salary range for your type of job in your region, you then have a good reason to request a raise.

There are several salary tracking websites that can connect you with the information and facts you need. When you have verified your realistic earnings potential, you then have a reasonable income goal in mind. I suggest you decide on an actual figure. As soon as that is established, you can arrange your plan to demand a reasonable raise.

Second, once you understand how much of a raise you want, you can start to equate that raise to the work that you do. Write everything down: how much work you do and what duties you are responsible for. All of this effort is part of explaining the wisdom of paying you more. Your job at this point is to prove to your employer that you see and understand their company's requirements, and that you work to be part of the solution. The point is not to just ask for money. It is to do so in a manner that confirms your value to the company how you contribute to its goals.

Once you can explain your value in fair and pragmatic terms, then you definitely are seen as an important part of their system.

In those cases, where you this type of immediate, open relationship with your employer does not exist yet, then you must - start by planning how to work with them more closely, so you can have their attention later to get your raise. Begin by planning a casual talk with your boss. Let him or her know you would like to help them to reach their business goals, and you would like to move ahead as well. Ask about the best ways to improve on current results.

For example, inquire from your manager precisely what you could do to add value to your results. Or, make inquiries about specific areas of professional or product development, while also paying attention to ways in which your employer could help.

Another technique would be to ask your boss straight away exactly what it would take to get a considerable raise in the next 5-6 months. The idea here is to identify the exact actions needed to achieve your raise in income, and then set those actions in motion. Decide, in actual detail, the amount of money you might earn when you get a raise. Once you have established your willingness to perform to some extent that justifies a raise in income, request the raise.

Importantly, your effort to justify a big raise for yourself is usually measured by how well you can get along with, and work with, others. This requires that you ask yourself some uncomfortable questions, and you'll need to be sincere in your answers. You must not be avoiding asking yourself about these core issues, even if the answers are difficult. Without this kind of self-knowledge, your efforts to ask for a raise will be wasted. For example, ask yourself precisely how you get along with your co-workers now? How do they perceive you? Precisely what would they say about you?

In addition, ask yourself the following questions: Do you show creativity in your work by accomplishing more than expected without having to be asked? Do you really respect the company you work for? Do you value and respect your boss? Are you thought of as a 'stand-out' or as a 'seldom-seen' worker? Do you have a vision for yourself and for the company or organization you work for that extends over the next three years? Assuming you have such a vision, are you ready to put that in writing? To put it another way, if your working habits and overall performance appear to be weak to other employees, you will have to fix those perceptions.

By having a plan for this conversation about a raise, you can influence the results positively. Once you are certain that your title or duties yield a higher earnings in your location, and that your past hard work has shown good results. and also benefited your co-workers too - that's when your employer will start to get seriously interested in giving you a raise. But make sure to bear this in mind; don't leave the results to chance. Ensure you always work hard to achieve them and make things happen. That's the reason why you choose to meet with your superior ahead of asking for a raise. You want their opinion about what can be done to improve your specific case. Include those actions in your strategy. This way, whenever you go in to request your raise, you are filled with self-confidence since you can point out definite goals and plans that your boss requested, and which you have also fulfilled.

Salesmen have a saying: "Ask for the order." More often than not, salesmen lose the potential sale simply because they do not convince the prospective buyer to make the purchase; the same exact situation exists when you want a raise.

Most times, people are scared to ask for more money. Employers like it this way. They expect you to be scared of demanding money. You have to break that this rule.

Once again: arrange and make a plan for the way you are going to request your raise. The best way would be to establish a follow-up visit with your boss, once you have the plan to get the raise, and after you've been able to highlight your efforts and bring them to the attention of your employer. After this, its relatively easy.

Clearly and concisely review with your employer the goals you have been given to achieve a raise. Be comprehensive. Provide reports to support your cause. Be persuasive and not possessive. Concentrate on your results and the anticipated raise figures which were discussed earlier.

Demanding a raise is challenging. On the other hand, you can find it easy; by simply following the suggestions given here, a contentedly employed person has a realistic possibility of a big raise in pay. Valued employees who request raises based on clear evidence of their value will succeed much more frequently.

We have provided several resources for market based data. This will help you as a guide to market salaries. There are no guarantees that you will succeed in getting a raise. Salary is a complex issue and dependent on several factors, primarily demand and supply.

Accounting

Robert Half International is a great site that provides data on comparative salaries for the Accounting, Finance and Tax professionals.

Simply Hired offers comparative salaries for many occupations. A comparative study was done on the salaries of accountants with startling results across America. They offer a wide range of information on the profession as a whole with comparative studies on the average salary for jobs with related titles. Some of the information you can find on Simply Hired is:

- Average yearly accounting salaries throughout the United States
- Links that let you compare salaries
- A link to current available jobs in accounting
- A salary calculator
- Links to jobs related to the field like bookkeeping
- Charts and graphs on the average salary in related fields

Administrative, Secretarial and Executive Assistant

USA Wage has information on salaries for executive secretaries and executive assistant salaries by state at the bottom of the page. They have information on the highest paying cities, and the highest paying industries. This is a pretty straight forward site. You just click on the state for the statistics. They also have information on:

- Hourly wages
- Yearly salaries
- Salary trends
- Related job salaries
- Salaries by city, county and area
- Percentile comparisons across the United States

Anesthesiologist

You can find valuable information about anesthesiology with a free membership to Medscape. They have news and perspectives on a variety of specialties. The compensation report for an anesthesiologist describes the productivity statistics, earnings and career satisfaction. They also offer links to other occupations within the medical physician industry and other information like:

- Procedures that deal with disease
- Calculators to determine the Glasgow Coma Scale and other stroke determiners and out comes
- Examination protocols
- Diagnostic imaging rules
- Diagnostic criteria
- Explore procedures
- A slide show collection
- Case studies
- Quizzes
- Trends in medicine

Astronaut

Universe Today has everything you need to know about astronauts. They have great pictures of astronauts in action from space agencies around the world. With interactive links for information on space and other planets, Universe Today is a fun way to search out a career as an astronaut. A few of the places you can follow them are Twitter, Facebook, YouTube and Instagram. Along with the average salaries for astronauts around the world, they also include:

- Videos of space
- How to become an astronaut?
- Biographies
- Astronaut salaries according to pay grade
- Active and training astronauts at NASA
- A discussion forum

Author and Writer

PayScale is a good place to look for salaries on any career. They allow you to search for similar jobs, what businesses should pay for different jobs and industries, and you can get a salary report. The article on author and writer salaries is full of information for writers and includes data like:

- Charts on salaries for related jobs
- A map with the pay difference by location
- Charts on pay by experience level
- Popular skills
- Job searches
- Health benefits
- Salary comparisons by gender
- Skills that affect a writers earning potential
- An interactive graph of common career paths
- A job description
- Common career goals
- Salaries by city and experience

Auto Mechanic

The occupational employment of automotive service technicians and mechanics was compiled by the United States Department of Labor and the Bureau of Labor Statistics in 2014. Information on overhauling automotive vehicles, diagnostic and repair for buses, trucks and diesel engine specialists is included in the report. The average yearly salary for an auto mechanic is shown by occupations within the industry in hourly and yearly rates. Other information also includes:

- Industry profiles
- A map of geographical salaries
- Salary comparison by state
- Top paying states
- Salaries by metropolitan area
- Areas with the highest paying jobs in automotive repair
- Occupation profiles

Biologist

Salary Explorer has done a salary comparison on all kinds of careers. They have links that let you compare your salary to other careers and resources for all careers. Their comparison survey covers the careers of biologists all over the United States with the average monthly and yearly salaries. You can take a job satisfaction survey and find general job statistics. More can be found about a career as a biologist, such as:

- Salary comparisons biologist vs technical and scientific services
- Salary comparison for all jobs
- Salary comparison by job title, such as microbiology, lab technician, chemist and a life scientist
- A salary comparison by job category
- Comparison by years of experience

Biochemist

Environmental Science has resources for environmental studies, degrees, policies and schools. They have a breakdown of the industry and include information like:

- What a biochemist is
- What a biochemist does
- Where a biochemist works
- Information on the different branches of biochemistry
- A comparative list of salaries by state
- Jobs
- Employment demand
- Earning a degree in biochemistry
- Degrees related to the industry
- Links to professional organizations and societies
- Related careers
- Information on internships
- Scholarship information
- Links to the top environmental schools

The Global Post is the leading America's world news site and has a list of salary ranges for research biochemists. They also have information on technology, politics, money and life. Their links on education, health and wellness, real estate, family and parenting give a wealth of good information. They offer information on topics, such as:

- The national average salary for a biochemist
- Wages by employment sector
- Wages by location
- The job outlook for biochemists
- A monthly newsletter
- Links to valuable information for the industry
- Links to the Bureau of Labor and Statistics

CEO

The Economic Policy Institute wrote an article on the comparative salaries for a CEO. The article centers on wage incomes and wealth across America. They give you the chance to subscribe to their newsletter and offer information on their areas of research, resources, publication and advice on different topics by experts. The article has information on the salary for a CEO like:

- Download a PDF of the article
- CEO compensation trends
- Stock price trends from 1965 to 2013
- Interactive graph on the S&P 500 index
- CEO compensation growth
- Trends for the CEO-to-worker ratio
- Chart on the growth of CEO and college wages

In April of 2014 The American Enterprise Institute (AEI) did a study on the average salary of a CEO for 2014. The report shows that the average salary of a CEO in the U.S. was $178,400 with a raise of less than 1 percent. They also give information about scholars, events and policy areas. They also offer information and links to academic programs, careers and internships. Some of the information offered in the article about CEO salaries includes:

- The annual average wage for a CEO in different professions
- A link to 27 million private sector firms
- A link to the Bureau of Labor Statistics annual report for occupational employment and wages
- An open discussion on CEO pay

Computer Scientists

Cornell University's Department of Computer Science did a comparative study on the average salary for a graduating computer scientist. The average salary across the board is $98,847. They listed the companies and locations in a chart. The site also offers information and links to seminars, lectures, events, a course list and is geared for placement information. You can also find information on:

- Career information
- Placement help
- Forms
- A quick chart
- Masters programs
- Schools
- Access to placement archives
- Alumni destinations

Court Personnel

United States Courts offers more information on law enforcement officers of the court salaries. They have information about the federal courts, judges and judgeships, court records, statistics and reports, business opportunities, services and forms and policies. The salaries are listed in a table by job description, state, rank and city. Some of the other information included:

- Job searches
- Benefits
- Compensation
- A glossary of legal terms
- Email updates
- Data tables
- Publications
- A frequently asked questions section
- A court locator
- News within the industry
- Career information about the industry

Corporate Communicators

The Public Relation Society brings this compilation of salary figures for <u>Corporate Communicators</u>. Their website relies on The Official PR Salary & Bonus Report released by Spring Associates. In addition to salary figures, the site offers education and career guidance in various branches of the public relations industry.

- Salary information by job title
- Limited geographic breakdown

Commercial Pilots

Compensation for a career as a <u>Commercial Pilot</u> is complex. It depends on a huge field of factors, divided across a wide spectrum of job titles. However, the Bureau of Labor Statistics does a great job of simplifying the data for viewers to understand. This allows for users to more easily find the information that they seek.

• Information on high paid geographic areas
• Averages broken down by specialization
• Quotient of persons holding job by state
• Salary by state
• Top paid metropolitan areas
• Top paying non-metropolitan areas
• Projections on estimated job growth and stability

No matter what the job, there are people interesting in exploring salary information. In fact, compensation is the biggest factor that people consider when deciding on a career. All of the sites that have been reviewed provided excellent information on salaries. Any one of them could be useful to career explorers old and young alike.

Dentists

The World Salaries website offers a comparative study on all kinds of different occupations. One report they did was an international study on what a dentist makes in a year. They also define how the information was gathered, and they include content like:

- The average salary for a dentist by country
- Links to the different countries labor statistics sites
- Information from the International Labor Organization
- Information on social security withholdings
- A link to the OECD Tax Database
- The Interbank nominal exchange rate
- A World Economic Outlook database
- A link to a database that shows information for taxes in different countries
- A gross income calculator table

Detectives

When it comes to getting salary information, the Bureau of Labor Statistics has the corner of the market for <u>Detectives and Criminal Investigators</u>. This particular career field is one of the most expansive on the list. This is why the Bureau of Labor Statistics is such a great fit. They present an impressive breakdown of information.

- Charts followed by informative maps
- Maps translate information into a geographic breakdown
- Top paying locations highlighted
- Career specializations and sectors presented

Elementary School Teachers

Business Insider provides useful information for elementary school teachers. The comparative salaries are done by state. You can follow them on Twitter and Facebook, find them on LinkedIn or send them an email. Some of the information offered at Business Insider is:

- Average salaries by state
- Colorful interactive maps
- A table showing the average salary
- Links on how much income is taxed around the world
- A video of different statistics around the world
- A link to National Teacher Appreciation Day
- Links to labor statistics
- The most up-to-date information of 2014
- A link for interactive maps and charts on the employment and yearly wages for preschool, primary school, middle school and secondary schools

Emergency Medical Technician

Top EMT Training has information about the field of emergency medical technician training. You can find a school and a program that fits your needs. They offer salary comparisons by state. On Top EMT Training you can find links that offer information on how to become an EMT, job descriptions and job duties for different occupations within the industry. They also include information on:

- Firefighter requirements
- Paramedic requirements
- Information on scholarships and grants
- Refresher courses
- Job outlooks
- Salaries of related job titles
- A practice test
- What an EMT makes yearly
- Average annual and yearly pay rates

Editors, Columnist and Reporters

Editors, Columnists and Reporters

This career field might encourage the imagination to conjure images of smoke filled news rooms, savvy ace reporters, and the sound of typewriters. However, the reality is a bit different. It involves long hours, deadlines, and lots of mental stress. Yet these jobs can be rewarding in financial and non-monetary terms. Regardless, this site offers a good coverage on salary information.

• Quick easy read
• Reduction of redundant information
• Salary information organized by job title
• Brief description of job
• Average salary amount presented

Faculty of Higher Education

Start Class comprised a list of average salaries for higher education faculty ranging from 9 months to a yearly comparison. They offer the salary information by university and allows you to compare it with other salaries in the profession. Public and private universities are listed. You can find more information on the comparative salary of the faculty in higher education with links, such as:

- School categories, including universities, associate's colleges, Liberal Arts Colleges and specialized institutions
- Academic rankings for instructors, lecturers, assistant professors, associate professors and professors
- Over 11,000 listing of salaries
- The ability to add your salary

Inside Higher Ed offers information on higher education salaries around the world. The site has links to a variety of useful information for anyone working in the field of higher education. Up-to-date news, career advice, technology, books, surveys, teaching, a current job listing and more on a global level. Their comparison studied the purchasing power and not pure salaries. Canada leads the way with the highest average salaries for those new to the academic profession. Also included are:

- A chart showing the average monthly salary from around the world
- A job board
- A link to the project's results
- Featured employers

FBI Agents

<u>Federal Law enforcement agents</u> adhere to the governments GS pay scale. Therefore, it is pretty standard across the board. However, there are some factors that differentiate salaries. The biggest factor is geographic location. Some cities offer a differential to the offset higher cost of living.

- Easy to follow charts
- Breakdown of geographic differentials
- Salary increases based on time on the job

Flight Attendants

Flight Attendants- There are an incredible amount of factors that affect earnings amount in this field. Travel is a large part of the job of a flight attendant. The switching between states, time zones, and countries means that a complex system of rate changes. This site does an excellent job of reducing this into a simple and easily navigable site.

• Base salary information
• Divided into international and domestic work zones
• Per diem information for layovers and in between stays
• Information taken from United Airlines Flight Attendants organization
• Simple chart design
• Site provides further data on career guidance and education programs

General Surgeon

Time did a comparative study of the yearly salaries of doctors at Healthandtime.com. They put together a comprehensive report on which surgeons make the most and which make the least. Time found that the average yearly salary for a general surgeon is well above six figures in 2011. Experience level and residency have a large impact on a surgeon's salary. The report includes things like:

- How the report was conducted?
- The average yearly salary of doctor's overall
- The average yearly salary for a specialty practice
- Discusses the difference in salaries between men and women who practice surgery
- Provide links to reports like the surgeon's health and happiness, the full Medscape
- Physician Compensation Report and an article on the push to reduce unnecessary tests

Government Jobs

In many areas, **Public** are the largest demographic. The debate about the benefits of public versus private sector employment is likewise immense. This site offers a well thought out and comprehensive comparison of these two career fields. However, it does tend to linger on the comparison to much. Yet, there is a lot of useful information.

- Discussion of differences of compensation
- Effects of perception of productivity
- in depth information, versus informatics

High School Teachers

The Bureau of Labor and Statistics compiled an occupation outlook handbook for high school teachers. This handbook offers a quick facts chart for high school teachers nationwide. This carries a lot of valuable information for the teaching profession. Some of the information you can find in this handbook is:

- Pay summary for the profession in 2012
- Information on how to become a high school teacher
- Information on similar jobs
- An alphabetical list of job outlooks
- The working environment
- What special qualifications a high school teacher needs
- Links for more information about teaching

Healthcare Careers

All Allied Health Schools is full of useful information for people working in the healthcare industry. You can explore careers like massage therapy, pharmacy, public health and veterinary medicine. They have information on different healthcare career salaries and popular jobs in the allied health field. Average yearly salaries are based on location, experience and occupation within the industry. They also offer information on things like:

- School listing
- Career advice
- Articles and resources
- Average yearly salaries for healthcare specialties
- Salaries for communication sciences
- Medical career salary comparisons
- Nursing salaries
- Imaging salary comparisons
- Salaries for physical therapists

Insurance Agents

U.S. News and World Report did another study on the comparative salaries of insurance agents. The site offers a job overview, salary information, reviews and advice and job listings by zip code. Insurance agents are listed as the number 7 top job in best businesses and are number 33 in the 100 best jobs. More information is included, such as:

- The overall score ranking for insurance agents
- The number of jobs
- The average salary
- The unemployment rate
- Salary range
- A link for a full report on salary data
- Training
- Reviews and advice
- Job satisfaction rates

Journalists

Poynter is a global leader for journalists and offers information on a wide range of journalistic topics. They have a rolling list of featured jobs within the industry. Along with salary comparisons, Poynter offers links for seminars, visual aids, quick tips for building skills, advice and story analysis. They talk about the job market and the future salaries of journalists. Information also included:

- The widening pay gap between reporters and PR specialists
- Map of average salaries by state
- States where journalists earn more than the average salary
- States where journalists earn less than the average salary
- Which states are the best and worst for journalism salaries

Lawyers

The ABA Journal is a great place to keep up on the newest trends within the legal system. In 2009, they teamed up with William Henderson, from the Center on the Global Legal Profession at Indiana University's Maurer School of Law and conducted a study of annual salaries for lawyers. The study found that the comparative salaries in the ever changing business of practicing law are dependent on years of experience and location. If you want to compare the salaries of lawyers, the ABA journal offers many visual aids, such as:

- The ability to search for salary information by country
- Colorful maps
- A search function for little known legal markets
- Graphs showing where law firm payrolls are the largest
- A chart indicating the cities where lawyers make the most income

Law school graduates

The National Association for Law Placement (NALP) offers a place for graduating law students to find jobs and compare salaries. The yearly salary for a new lawyer varies from state to state and county to county. The site is a great place to determine where you want to start your practice and offers a search for information like:

- Private sector salaries
- A salary distribution curve
- Public sector salaries
- A workplace questionnaire analysis
- A member salary survey, this is password protected
- The starting salaries based on years of experience
- A report of salaries by city, firm size and full or part-time employment

Life Insurance Agents

Bank rate gives information on a variety of topics along with the salaries for life insurance agents like bank rates, identity protection advice, personal loan information, mortgage rates and insurance. This article centers on how much a life insurance agent can make. It includes information like:

- Commissions
- Links to review quotes
- Advice on how to make the sale
- An open discussion on life insurance
- Rate calculators
- Advice on retirement
- Advice on financial planning
- The ability to find and compare the lowest insurance quotes from the top companies

Lead Foreman and Construction Workers

Once again, Simply Hired has done a great job of putting together a list of comparative salaries for foreman and construction workers. They give you the opportunity to search for jobs by salary and location. They have searches for salary comparisons by keywords and location. The average salary for lead foreman jobs was calculated with the average salary for jobs with the search term "lead foreman". Other information included:

- Average salary for jobs with related titles
- Salary information for a lead foreman
- A salary calculator
- Job searches
- A link to other salary searches
- Job trends

Law Enforcement

At Law Enforcement EDU you have the chance to search for police officer jobs, sheriff jobs and deputy sheriff employment. They discuss the factors that influence law enforcement salaries, and they discuss the possibilities of earning a six figure income after years of experience. Other information they include:

- A list of comparative salaries by state
- Bonus opportunities
- Links to find a good school
- A blog
- Police officer resources
- Law enforcement resources

Mathematicians

The American Mathematical Society (AMS) does an annual comprehensive study of the average salaries for a mathematician. They looked at all the data and compiled a list of tenure-track faculty and faculty members within the United States. The list is broken down by year and goes as far back as 1999. Other information found at AMS includes:

- A calendar of events
- Member journals
- News within the industry
- Quick links to surveys, graduate programs and department groups
- Career information
- Employment services
- Data on starting salaries
- Data on faculty salaries
- Prizes and awards for mathematicians
- Grants and opportunities

Medical Scientist

The United States Department of Labor put together an occupational handbook for the medical scientist. They offer links and summaries of what a medical scientist does, their work environment, how to become a medical scientist, the job outlook and information for similar occupations. Other information offered in the handbook includes:

- Average annual salaries for jobs within the industry
- Industries at a glance link
- Economic releases
- Maps
- Databases and tables
- A calculator for inflation
- Tutorials
- Information on careers
- Information for students
- Benefits
- Unemployment
- Employment projections

Medical Field

AOL Jobs is in a partnership with CareerBuilder to help you search for job opportunities in the medical field. You can search for jobs, get hired, find news on the industry, stories and videos. They have searches for the top 10 highest paying jobs, and they list salaries by job description. Also included are links to:

- Companies hiring this week
- A job hunter check list
- Best cities to start a medical career
- Government jobs
- Top jobs for people over 50
- Best and worst jobs of the year

Miscellaneous

Top Ten Reviews is a good place to find a job, get statistics on the jobs with the highest satisfaction and review course studies and requirements for working within the industry. They have featured articles, reviews and software tools you can use to help you find employment and discover new trends in the industry. Salaries are listed from highest to lowest wages and by occupation. You can also look for information about services like business, science techs, electronics and auto techs. They also include things like:

- A free newsletter
- Interactive charts that compare medical careers
- Links to educational requirements
- Links to job availability for each occupation
- Work environments
- Colorful, easy to read charts and graphs

Marketing

All Business Schools offers salary comparisons by the occupations in marketing. They talk about career choices, earning potential, career demand and job growth within the field. At All Business Schools you can find information on schools, and they have links for articles on finding the right business career for you. They also offer things like:

- How to advance your marketing career?
- The companies that hire marketers
- How much competition you will face
- A marketing career guide
- An educational degree guide

Makeup Artists

Beauty centered careers on the rise, especially in recent years. Like a lot of growing fields this is because of the necessity that everyone has for it. T his site offers a comprehensive overview of the industry. Again statistics from the Bureau of Labor Statistics were utilized.

- Annual salary information
- Hourly wage information
- Separated into percentiles; 10th. 25th, 50th, 75th, and 90th
- Information on the highest paid geographic location
- Easily read charts
- Organized into logical short paragraphs
- Career centered education advice

Meteorologist

Each year <u>Meteorologists</u> from all over the country gather to attend the American Meteorological Society's broadcast conference. Information is compiled from confidential surveys taken at the conference. This site, along with wxsurvey.com, offer a great presentation of the data retrieved from this survey. That information can be extremely helpful to job explorers as well as those already working as broadcast meteorologists.

• Salary information divided by relevant factors that affect earnings
• Time of broadcast is the largest of these factors
• Easy to read charts and graphics
• Each image accompanied with a detailed analysis of the presented data
• Rest of the site is a tremendous resource for entry level broadcast
meteorologist

Neuroscientist

Salary Genius has a tool that allows you to find a school
and get information on different programs as well as a
comparative study for salaries as a neuroscientist by state.
You can search for a profession, browse professions and
find a school of your choice. Each state is broken down into
salaries by county, city and zip code. More information on
the salaries for a neuroscientist also includes:

- Similar professions
- Job interview tips
- Top 20 questions asked by job interviewers
- Salary tools
- Similar salaries
- National salary data
- Search career salaries alphabetically

Nursing

All Nursing Schools has a comprehensive list of salaries for registered nurses by employers, educational background, experience and specialty. At AllNursingSchools.com you can explore careers and degrees from entry level to advanced training. Other information also included is:

- Links to find a program that fits you
- How to advance your career?
- Who hires registered nurses
- Job growth
- Salary comparisons based on specialty
- Information on the difference between a registered nurse (RN) and a licensed vocational nurse (LVN)
- Earning potential
- School listings
- Answers to common questions

News Anchors

Salary.com is a premier site for career exploration for <u>News Anchors</u> . This article does not disappoint. It offers a great presentation of relevant job information. Salary information comes from a study by the University of Missouri's Journalism School. Organization of that data is well handled and presented in an informative manner.

• General overview of salary information
• Data presented in simple paragraph form
• Divided into market size
• Average salary amounts in each market
• Relevant career information from CNN's Jonathan Mann

Orthodontist

The United Stated Department of Labor puts out a report every year for the comparative salaries for the orthodontic profession. They compile information from the The Bureau of Labor Statistics and put it all in one convenient location. Information about yearly salaries for orthodontist also includes:

- Colorful maps and charts of data from different states
- Maps and charts of data for cities
- The average salary for an orthodontist from state to state
- The occupational employment statistics
- Links for information on data
- An overview of the site
- Publications and news releases
- Occupational profiles
- Technical notes

The Dental Career Guide is a good quick source of information about the yearly salaries for orthodontists. They offer information on how an orthodontist can work for another dentist or open their own practice. The data is arranged by state, and includes information like:

- The state
- How many orthodontists are employed in that state?
- The average hourly wage
- The average yearly wage
- Updates
- News in dentistry
- Links to the top jobs for orthodontists
- The ability to check the license of a dentist
- Voting polls on the dentistry profession

Oncologists

Medscape is a very comprehensive and versatile site. It is intended as a reference site for medical professionals. That reference extends to career resources as well as medication information. The site does require membership registration in order to view their articles. However, the process is simple and takes relatively little time.

• Visually simple, interactive charts and graphs
• Data divided by geographic location, specialty, and certification

Pediatrician

The Bureau of Labor Statistics is one of the best places to go for salary comparison information. They have the most up to date information out there. Conducting a statistical search, they compared the salaries of pediatricians across the United States with information like:

- A geographic profile
- National estimates
- An industry profile
- A color coded map of the states with the highest employment level
- Charts and color maps that show how many pediatricians are employed, an average hourly rate and a yearly salary by state
- Links to places that give information like occupation profiles, wage estimates by state and national wage estimates

Programmers

Stackoverflow does a study on comparative salaries for programmers around the world every year. The study done in 2015 gives a lot of information on the programming industry as a whole. This study comes with overviews on technology, work and the industry community. Some of the information you can find includes:

- Average compensation by technology
- Average compensation by purchasing power
- Employment status
- Job satisfaction statistics
- Information about the industry
- Information on developers
- A survey on the industry
- Charts and graphs on percentages globally
- Trivial facts about programmers

Psychiatrist

You need to create a free account for Medscape before you can access their information on salaries. Once you become a member, you have access to everything on the site. They offer information on:

- Drugs
- Diseases
- News
- Perspectives
- Continuing education
- Continuing medical education for physicians
- Information on different specialties
- Breaking medical news
- Clinical perspectives
- Access to free mobile and online references
- Professional development courses
- Links to Medscape Deutschland
- Links to Medscape France
- A link to WebMD
- A link to WebMD's corporate office

Plumber

ePlumbing Courses is a great place for plumbers to find everything they need to know about the industry. At ePlumbing Courses you can find a school, and they offer quick facts on the industry. Salaries are broken down into categories by location, years of experience and title. At ePlumbing Courses you can find out where and what you need to begin a career as a plumber, advice on how to pick a school and get information on each state's license and training requirements. Some of the other things they include are:

- A career path
- Interview tips
- Job listings
- Apprenticeships
- Plumbing courses
- An employment outlook

Paralegals

Certified Paralegal

This community based site is a goldmine of information about a career as a paralegal. Its salary information is based upon information from the 2006 and 2009 Annual Compensation Survey for Paralegals. Further data comes from the Bureau of Labor Statistics. It breaks down that survey's data into easy to navigate categories.

• Salary by region
• Salary by specialty; government, corporate, legal, and etc.
• Career growth projection
• Highlights of highest paid geographic areas
• Easily understandable tables, graphs, and charts.

Project Managers

<u>Project Managers</u>

The fate of project managers in the wake of the 2009 financial crisis seems to be fair. At least that is what The Project Management Institute has revealed in its salary survey. Data from that survey is compiled on this site in an easy to ready paragraph form. There are no fancy graphics, just straight numbers and facts. However, the organization is extremely helpful.

Salary Information based on
• Certification
• Gender
• Industry
• Size of team
• Project type
• Education

Record company Jobs

Record company jobs is actually a blanket term that covers a wide range of jobs. From the person that acquires new musical talent to the campus intern that hands out promotional flyers on the quad. The range of salaries are also expansive. This site provides a great overview of every job on this vast range.

• Earnings information divided into separate job title sections
• Short job description
• Alternate title names
• Average salary range data
• Easy search feature allows user to navigate to desired title

Sales representatives

U.S. News and Money does a good comparative study on the occupation of being a sales representative. They offer good information on careers, personal finances, investments and retirement. Under the career search, they let you find information about the top jobs and salaries in the United States. They include information like:

- A job overview
- Reviews and advice
- Job listings
- Average salaries
- Sales representative pay compared to other professions
- Which are the best paying cities
- Colorful charts and graphs comparing salaries
- Links to salaries and benefits
- A link to find an online degree program

The Glass Door is a no frills place to find information on comparative salaries for a sales representative by company. They also offer information on salaries by job category and give people the opportunity to add their salary anonymously. If you find a job that interests you, they let you upload your résumé. At the Glass Door you can also find information like:

- Pages of salary information by company
- The opportunity to get email updates on jobs in your area
- Search jobs by title
- Search yearly salaries by job title
- Information on different types of sales rep job like retail, territory, field sales and pharmaceutical sales

Statistician

Sokanu has information on all aspects of a career as a statistician. They offer data on careers, degrees, the industry and finance along with a comparative analysis of the average salary by state. With an overview on how to become a statistician, a history of past salaries, links to the job market and they answer questions, this site is a wealth of information. Also included on the site is:

- An interactive career test to see if being a statistician would be a good fit
- Starting average salary through the highest paid
- A color map of salaries by state
- A chart with each state's rank and salary with links to each
- Job listings
- Information on careers in general with salary comparisons

Scientist /Master of Science Degree

The Statistic Brain Research Institute has an hourly and an average yearly wage listed for a scientist. They offer information on percentages and rankings. Their source is the U.S. Bureau of Labor Statistics resources from 2012. The average salary for a scientist is broken down by occupation. Along with the comparison study on salaries, you can also find statistical information on:

- Companies
- Education
- Marketing
- Health
- Crime
- The financial industry
- Technology
- Media
- Food
- People
- The government
- Demographics
- Sports
- People
- A subscription to their YouTube
- The digital magazine industry
- Student loan debt
- Business funding sources

PayScale Human Capital has done a great study on comparative salaries for anyone with a master of science degree. They allow you to track the average salary ranges by job. With links on salaries by the hour, bonuses, popular tallies and more, you will find everything you need to know about being a scientist at PayScale. You can search by years of experience, job, company size, certification and by city, or state. More information attainable at PayScale is:

- A salary report by location and years of experience
- Colorful graphs and charts
- Statistics based on gender
- Popular cities
- Schools
- Career tips and advice
- Job satisfaction rates
- Which companies are popular

System Analyst

IT Career Finder has a lot of good information on system analyst. They offer links and information on IT careers, certifications and training in the industry. They give you the option of exploring a career path in system analysis and salary information on different aspects of the job, such as database administrator, web developer, designers, security analyst and computer systems. There is a computer system analysts starting salary history for the past 3 years in related professions. Other information you can find at IT Career Finder includes:

- A search for schools
- What percentage to add to salaries for different skills
- Comparative salaries by state
- Top 10 highest paying jobs in the industry
- Salary comparisons by experience, industry and specialty
- Other IT job functions compared to the wages of a system analysis
- Links for training

Social Worker

The Social Work Career Center lets you search for a job, explore the social worker profession and explore employers. They have links for education, training and career development. Find salaries bases on a geographic location, highest to lowest, degree and gender. They also offer information and links for things like:

- Posting a résumé
- Finding a job
- Building a résumé
- Get interview tips
- Review practice interview questions
- Advice on how to market yourself
- Fast facts on social worker salaries
- Earnings from the National Study of Licensed Social Workers
- Data on the workforce

Stock Brokers

Information on <u>Stock Brokers</u> as a career can be a bit tricky. Stock Brokerage work is manly a sales occupation. Therefore, they rely heavily on commissions and bonuses. This site compiles the basic salary information from the Bureau of Labor Statistics.

• Salary information by state
• Then broken down by metropolitan area
• Information on size of field in that area
• Career projection
• Additional information about related careers; financial planning and advising

State Jobs

Expanding on the previous job category, this site takes it to the State level. However, unlike the federal level state government employees face some unique challenges. Yet, the career is very rewarding. The Pew Charitable Trusts offers a wonderful analysis of state workers' salaries.

• Easy to navigate interface
• Map view that breaks down state by state comparison
• Option to toggle between private and public sector jobs
• Per state median income
• Ability to perform an historic comparison of previous years

Teachers

The Institute of Education and Science (IES) Digest of Education Statistics has put together a table on the comparative salaries for teachers. They offer statistics and tables for every year dating back to 1969 with charts and figures. You can also look at the most recent issue of the Digest. This chart was put together in 2013, and shows every state average salary for a teacher. Also included are:

- Salaries by state
- Percentage changes over the years
- An Excel download of the chart
- Publications and products

- Fast facts
- School searches
- News and events
- Surveys and programs

Thank You!

I hope you've enjoyed this, the Second in the Quick Guide Series and you're armed with ideas to get real savings out of everyday spending!

With the quick links below you'll be able to rate this book, Tweet, and brag about it on Facebook. Please take a moment to do that. I'd very grateful and it will help others who are always looking for ideas for savings.

One last thing!

If you enjoyed this book or found it useful, I'd be very grateful if you'd post a short review on Amazon. Your support really does make a difference. I read all the reviews and strive to make it better based on your feedback.

All you need to do is click the link below that will take you directly to the review page in Amazon.

Many thanks and have a wonderful journey on savings

William

Tap here to go to my Amazon Author page and rate/review this e-book

Click here to review this book

Check out other books in this series

Tweet about this book

Post to Facebook

Savings Made Easy

This knuckle-whitening Resource Guide is now free for a limited time - you just need to tell me where to send it

Actual ideas on how I saved $3K in 2015 by following these tips. It does not take too long. Build your nest egg, pay bills , by using these tips - Savings without sacrifice! Check Out the Resource Guide FREE and implement Today! You may be leaving money on the table by not implementing these tips!

Read the Resource Guide Free -Then decide whether this is for you

Send My Free Book!

★★★★★   ★★★★★

"Savings Made Easy by William J King is a practical and easy to follow guide on how to spend less money while living exactly the same lifestyle you are accustomed to" Reviewed by Faridah Nassozi or Reader's Favorite

" The Best savings on everyday stuff " advice you're ever gonna get by Dr. Arti Easwar

Made in the USA
Columbia, SC
02 March 2020

88616722R00046